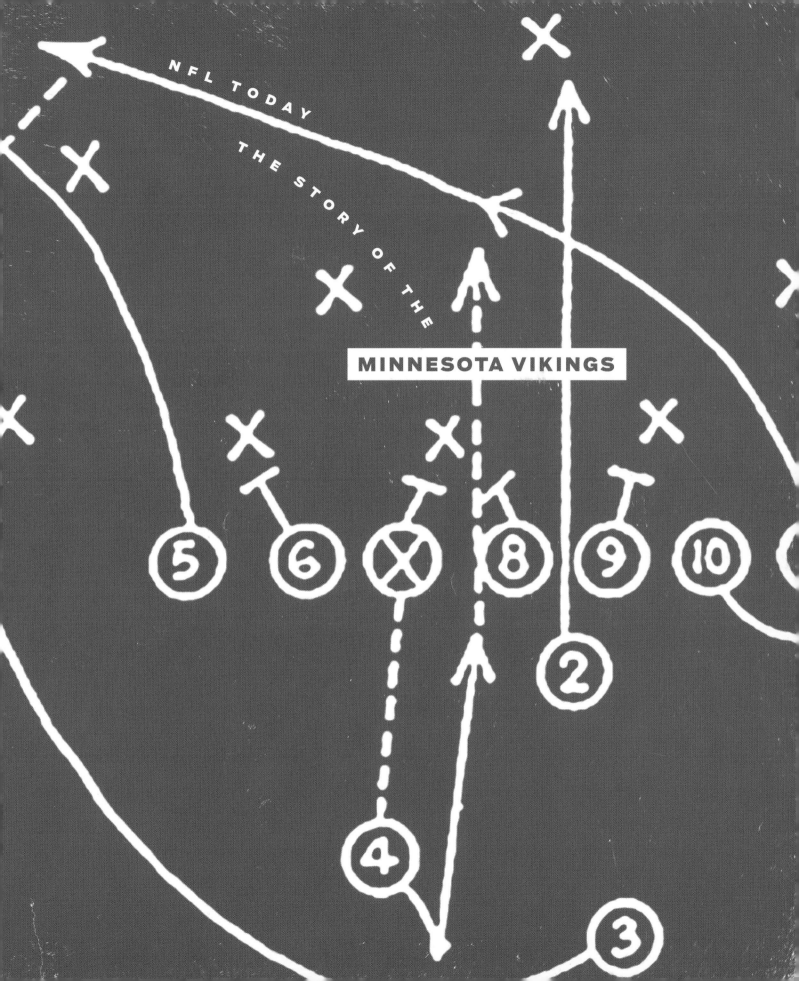

NFL TODAY

THE STORY OF THE

MINNESOTA VIKINGS

NFL TODAY

THE STORY OF THE MINNESOTA VIKINGS

SARA GILBERT

CREATIVE EDUCATION

PUBLISHED BY CREATIVE EDUCATION
P.O. BOX 227, MANKATO, MINNESOTA 56002
CREATIVE EDUCATION IS AN IMPRINT OF THE CREATIVE COMPANY
WWW.THECREATIVECOMPANY.US

DESIGN AND PRODUCTION BY BLUE DESIGN
ART DIRECTION BY RITA MARSHALL
PRINTED IN THE UNITED STATES OF AMERICA

PHOTOGRAPHS BY AP PHOTO (TOM OLMSCHEID),
GETTY IMAGES (BRIAN BAHR, ANDREW D. BERNSTEIN,
ADAM BETTCHER, RYAN BEYER, VERNON BIEVER/
NFL, MARK BRETTINGEN, PAUL BUCK/AFP, TOM
DAHLIN, JONATHAN DANIEL/ALLSPORT, JIM DAVIS/
BOSTON GLOBE, TOM DIPACE/SPORTS ILLUSTRATED,
STEPHEN DUNN, JAMES FLORES/NFL PHOTOS, FOCUS
ON SPORT, DREW HALLOWELL, TOM HAUCK, KIDWILER
COLLECTION/DIAMOND IMAGES, ANDY LYONS, ANDY
LYONS/ALLSPORT, JOHN MABANGLO/AFP, MARTIN
MILLS, RONALD C. MODRA/SPORTS IMAGERY, MARTIN
MORROW/NFL PHOTOS, MIKE NELSON/AFP, NFL,
ROBERT SULLIVAN/AFP)

LIBRARY OF CONGRESS CATALOGING-IN-PUBLICATION DATA
GILBERT, SARA.
THE STORY OF THE MINNESOTA VIKINGS / SARA GILBERT.
P. CM. — (NFL TODAY)
INCLUDES INDEX.
SUMMARY: THE HISTORY OF THE NATIONAL FOOTBALL LEAGUE'S
MINNESOTA VIKINGS, SURVEYING THE FRANCHISE'S BIGGEST
STARS AND MOST MEMORABLE MOMENTS FROM ITS INAUGURAL
SEASON IN 1961 TO TODAY.
ISBN 978-1-60818-309-8
1. MINNESOTA VIKINGS (FOOTBALL TEAM)—HISTORY—JUVENILE
LITERATURE. I. TITLE.

GV956.M5G55 2013
796.332'6409776579—DC23   2012031649

FIRST EDITION
9 8 7 6 5 4 3 2 1

COVER: RUNNING BACK ADRIAN PETERSON
PAGE 2: DEFENSIVE END JARED ALLEN
PAGES 4—5: MINNESOTA VIKINGS IN SUPER BOWL IV
PAGE 6: DEFENSIVE END JIM MARSHALL

TABLE OF CONTENTS

MINNEAPOLIS MAKES UP ONE HALF OF MINNESOTA'S "TWIN CITIES"

Vikings Set Sail

Minnesota is known as the Land of 10,000 Lakes—although that nickname doesn't quite do the state's landscape justice. There are almost 12,000 lakes larger than 10 acres within its borders and many more that aren't quite that big. More than 1,000 of those lakes are part of the Minneapolis-St. Paul metropolitan area, which explains how Minneapolis, which means "city of lakes," earned its name. It also helps explain why Minnesotans enjoy spending so much time outdoors despite living in the coldest major metro area in the United States.

Although many Minnesotans spend their free time boating, fishing, skiing, or otherwise enjoying the state's beautiful woods and water, others enjoy watching their favorite sports teams, indoors or out. They cheer for the Minnesota Timberwolves and the Minnesota Lynx, both professional basketball teams, for the Minnesota Wild professional hockey team, and for the Minnesota Twins major-league baseball team. And since 1961, they've spent most Sundays during the fall and winter rooting for their

THE VIKINGS' DEFENSIVE LINEMEN HAVE HISTORICALLY BEEN TOUGH

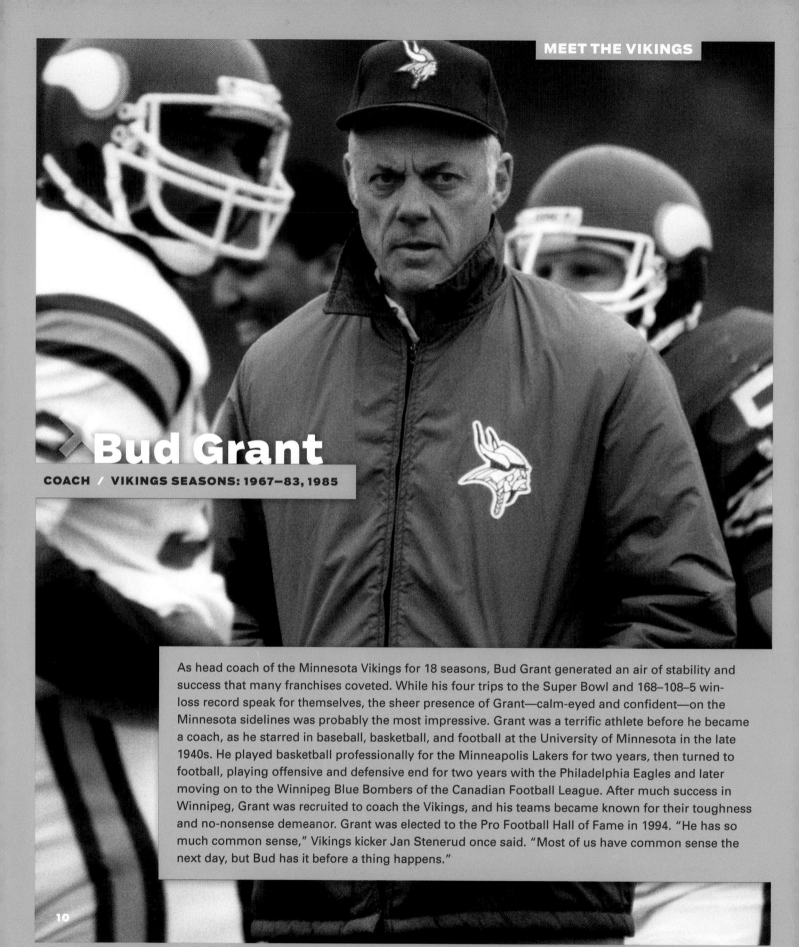

Bud Grant

COACH / VIKINGS SEASONS: 1967–83, 1985

As head coach of the Minnesota Vikings for 18 seasons, Bud Grant generated an air of stability and success that many franchises coveted. While his four trips to the Super Bowl and 168–108–5 win-loss record speak for themselves, the sheer presence of Grant—calm-eyed and confident—on the Minnesota sidelines was probably the most impressive. Grant was a terrific athlete before he became a coach, as he starred in baseball, basketball, and football at the University of Minnesota in the late 1940s. He played basketball professionally for the Minneapolis Lakers for two years, then turned to football, playing offensive and defensive end for two years with the Philadelphia Eagles and later moving on to the Winnipeg Blue Bombers of the Canadian Football League. After much success in Winnipeg, Grant was recruited to coach the Vikings, and his teams became known for their toughness and no-nonsense demeanor. Grant was elected to the Pro Football Hall of Fame in 1994. "He has so much common sense," Vikings kicker Jan Stenerud once said. "Most of us have common sense the next day, but Bud has it before a thing happens."

QUARTERBACK FRAN TARKENTON EXCELLED AS BOTH A PASSER AND A RUNNER

favorite National Football League (NFL) franchise, the Minnesota Vikings.

Given the climate in Minnesota, it is fitting that the Vikings' history began with a man named Winter—Max Winter. In the late 1950s, the Minnesota businessman began writing letters to the NFL commissioner, requesting permission to establish a football team in his home state. In 1960, the league finally gave him the go-ahead, and the Vikings were born.

Winter hired former NFL quarterback Norm Van Brocklin as the team's first head coach and assembled a roster that was made up mostly of unproven rookies and veterans cast off by other teams. Among the veterans was former San Francisco 49ers star running back Hugh McElhenny, and the group of rookies included cornerback Ed Sharockman and quarterback Fran Tarkenton.

Expectations weren't high for the first-year Vikings in 1961, but Minnesota surprised its fans and its opponents by crushing the Chicago Bears 37–13 in its first game. In the victory, Tarkenton proved himself a rising star by passing for four touchdowns and running for another. The Vikings went 3–11 that first season and posted losing records the next two seasons as well, but Tarkenton's scrambling style never

"Why should I stand there and get broken in two?"

FRAN TARKENTON

failed to thrill fans—and irritate his old-fashioned coach. Tarkenton had his reasons for darting around in the backfield. "Why should I stand there and get broken in two?" he once said. "If I run, there's always a chance that I will find a receiver."

While the Vikings' offense showed promise, the defense needed work. One of the few bright spots was defensive end Don Hultz. In 1963, the rookie earned league-wide attention by recovering nine opponents' fumbles—an NFL single-season record. His Vikings teammates began calling him "The Magnet" and were disappointed when he was traded away to make room in the lineup for Carl Eller, another outstanding young defensive end. Eller joined a line already anchored by 6-foot-4 and 248-pound Jim Marshall. Marshall spent 19 seasons with the Vikings and played in 282 consecutive games—an NFL record that would stand for almost four decades. Although his career featured countless highlights, many fans will always remember an infamous "lowlight" from 1964. In a game against the 49ers, Marshall scooped up a fumble and, momentarily confused, raced the wrong direction into the end zone, giving the 49ers two points for a safety.

With the emergence of tough running backs Bill Brown and Tommy Mason, center Mick Tinglehoff, and kicker Fred Cox, the Vikings improved to 8–5–1 in 1964. Then problems developed on the sidelines, where Coach Van Brocklin and Tarkenton often clashed. Following a 4–9–1 season in 1966, Van Brocklin became even more agitated with Tarkenton's maverick style. "There are two types of quarterbacks—those who carry a team and those who have to be carried by the team," the coach said. "Francis will win some games he shouldn't win, but he'll lose some games he shouldn't lose." Their public disputes ended in 1967, when Tarkenton was traded away to the New York Giants for four draft picks and cash, and Van Brocklin resigned.

Max Winter chose Bud Grant as the team's next head coach. A former football and baseball standout at the University of Minnesota—and a former coach in the Canadian Football League—Grant was just the patient, determined leader the Vikings needed. A tall, stern figure with a steely gaze, he would remain the face of the Minnesota Vikings for 18 seasons.

In 1968, Grant and the Vikings won their first and only NFL Western Conference Central Division title with an 8–6 record. Part of the credit went to scrappy signal-caller Joe Kapp, who steadied the

Like the Vikings

Hundreds of years ago, fierce warriors from the northern parts of Europe piled into long, narrow wooden boats, dipped their oars into the salty ocean water, and sailed away in search of treasure. Those warriors were known as Vikings, and their brutish behavior as they raided villages looking for gold, jewels, and other riches earned them a reputation as an aggressive, punishing bunch. When Bert Rose was named the first general manager of the new NFL franchise in Minnesota, he thought that rough-and-tumble image would fit the team well, especially because it was based in an area almost as cold and snowy as the Vikings' Scandinavian roots—and because many Minnesotans traced their heritage to the same region. Rose recommended that the board of directors choose Vikings as the team's name rather than one of the other suggestions before them—which included Miners, Chippewas, and Voyageurs. The board agreed that the name would imbue the new team's identity with a sense of strength and a will to win. Rose also recommended that the team colors be purple and gold, a suggestion that had more to do with the colors of his alma mater, the University of Washington in Seattle, than anything else.

THREE "PURPLE PEOPLE EATERS": JIM MARSHALL, CARL ELLER, AND ALAN PAGE

Vikings' attack with more traditional quarterback play; safety Paul Krause, who guided the defense with his on-field smarts and seven interceptions; and rookie Bobby Bryant, who made a solid impression at cornerback and would remain in the Vikings' defensive backfield for the next 13 seasons.

But the brightest stars were on the defensive line. Made up of ends Marshall and Eller and tackles Alan Page and Gary Larsen, Minnesota's line was among the NFL's best. All four players were amazingly quick and relentless in their pursuit. This fearsome front four, which became known as the "Purple People Eaters," followed a simple game plan: "Meet at the quarterback."

Alan Page

DEFENSIVE TACKLE / VIKINGS SEASONS: 1967–78 / HEIGHT: 6-FOOT-4 / WEIGHT: 245 POUNDS

It took only four games for Alan Page to win a starting role at defensive tackle with the Minnesota Vikings in his rookie season. For the next 12 seasons, Page never looked back, stuffing ballcarriers and sacking quarterbacks with his nimbleness and a game built on quickness and smarts. In 1971, Page became just the second defensive player in NFL history to win the league's Most Valuable Player (MVP) award. That season, Page recorded 9 sacks and 65 tackles and generally terrorized opposing offenses. Page was also a four-time Defensive Player of the Year in the National Football Conference (NFC), and along with fellow "Purple People Eaters" Jim Marshall and Carl Eller, he helped the Vikings reach four Super Bowls from 1970 to 1977. For his career, he blocked an incredible 28 kicks and recovered 23 fumbles. Page became a shining role model for ex-athletes when he retired from football, gained a law degree, and in 1992 was elected as an Associate Justice of the Minnesota Supreme Court, becoming the first African American to ever serve on that court. He was re-elected in 1998, 2004, and 2010.

Wrong Way Jim

When Minnesota Vikings defensive end Jim Marshall got spun around and rambled for his famous "Wrong Way Run," dizzy people everywhere could relate. "Think of the worst thing you've ever done," said Marshall, "the thing you're most ashamed of—and it was seen by 80 million people. Then think of people coming up to you and reminding you of it for the rest of your life." The scene of Marshall's folly was San Francisco, California, in a game against the 49ers, on October 25, 1964. Marshall scooped up a 49ers fumble and, disoriented, began to hoof it in the wrong direction. Some of Marshall's Vikings teammates pursued him but couldn't catch up or get his attention. Marshall sprinted into the 49ers' end zone and celebrated his jaunt by happily winging the ball into the stands. The resulting safety cost the Vikings two points, but Marshall offset the mistake by causing another 49ers fumble that the Vikings returned for a touchdown in a 27–22 victory. What's more, Marshall would eventually become the all-time NFL leader in opponents' fumble recoveries, with 29.

JIM MARSHALL PLAYED IN THE NFL FOR 20 SEASONS, STARTING EVERY GAME

The Golden (and Purple) Years

In 1969, the Vikings set sail for greatness. Kapp torched the Baltimore Colts with an NFL-record seven touchdown passes in the second game of the season. Then the Vikings won 11 games in a row before beating the Cleveland Browns 27–7 in the NFL Championship Game to win their first league title. As NFL champs, the Vikings then took on the Kansas City Chiefs of the rival American Football League (AFL) in Super Bowl IV. (Prior to the 1970 season, when the AFL and NFL merged, the NFL champs played the AFL champs in the Super Bowl.) The Vikings were heavily favored, but they could never get their offense going and lost, 23–7.

Despite the upset in Super Bowl IV, the good times were just beginning in Minnesota. The Vikings ruled the new National Football Conference (NFC) Central Division throughout the 1970s, winning the division eight times. In 1972, to the delight of many fans, Tarkenton returned and

EVEN KICKERS HAD A TOUGH TIME FACING THE PURPLE PEOPLE EATERS

Fran Tarkenton

QUARTERBACK / VIKINGS SEASONS: 1961–66, 1972–78 / HEIGHT: 6 FEET / WEIGHT: 185 POUNDS

In the first game in Minnesota Vikings history, Fran Tarkenton, a wiry rookie quarterback from Georgia, came off the bench to sling four touchdowns and run for a fifth as the Vikings toppled the Chicago Bears, 37–13. Tarkenton made a name for himself as a scrambling renegade whose dazzling escapes from the clutches of would-be tacklers had fans holding their breath. Not that he never took a hit. "It's kind of peaceful down there," Tarkenton said about occasionally ending up underneath a pile of tacklers. "It's a good time to be planning your next play." In 1967, Minnesota traded its star to the New York Giants. However, the Vikings reacquired Tarkenton in 1972. Tarkenton's second tour of duty for the purple and gold was much more successful, as he led the Vikings to three Super Bowls before he retired. After 18 seasons of football, Tarkenton was the all-time NFL leader in the most significant passing categories, including touchdowns (342), completions (3,686), and yards (47,003). He also rushed for 3,674 yards in his career, easily the best ever for a quarterback at that time.

"The greatest quarterback ever in the NFL."

BUD GRANT ON
FRAN TARKENTON

resumed scrambling across the frozen turf of Metropolitan Stadium. In 1975, Tarkenton—whom Grant called "the greatest quarterback ever in the NFL"—threw 25 touchdown passes and was named the league's MVP. With Tarkenton, running back Chuck Foreman, and wide receiver John Gilliam leading a strong offense, and with the Purple People Eaters continuing to devour opponents, the Vikings went 45–10–1 from 1973 to 1976 and returned to the Super Bowl three times. Sadly, the biggest prize of all eluded them, as they lost each time.

In 1975, the Vikings might have had their best squad of the era, going 12–2 in the regular season. Although it was heavily favored to reach the Super Bowl, Minnesota lost 17–14 to the Dallas Cowboys in the NFC playoffs when Cowboys receiver Drew Pearson hauled in a 50-yard scoring bomb from quarterback Roger Staubach with just 24 seconds remaining. The Vikings, and many Minnesota fans, contended that Pearson illegally pushed off of Vikings cornerback Nate Wright, and replays showed they might have been correct in their grievance.

As the 1970s drew to a close, the Vikings were haunted by their Super Bowl losses: 23–7 to Kansas City in Super Bowl IV; 24–7 to the Miami Dolphins in Super Bowl VIII; 16–6 to the Pittsburgh Steelers in Super Bowl IX; and 32–14 to the Oakland Raiders in Super Bowl XI. Although they would come close, the Vikings would not return to the Super Bowl during the next three decades.

It was clear that the team's talent was aging, but the great Vikings players who had tasted success in the '70s were able to put together a memorable moment in the second-to-last game of the 1980 season. The Vikings needed a win over the Cleveland Browns to capture the NFC Central. Down 23–22, Minnesota had the ball at midfield; quarterback Tommy Kramer launched a hopeful pass toward the end

Cold-Field Advantage

Many people can't stand the cold weather in the state of Minnesota. The Minnesota Vikings, early in their history, used that to their advantage. From 1961 to 1981, when the weather turned cold, the Vikings were nearly unstoppable as icy winds and freezing temperatures blew through Metropolitan Stadium. Their coach, Bud Grant, made sure they were ready for the cold by always making the team practice outdoors and prohibiting certain comforts such as heaters or gloves. The result was an emphatic home-field advantage that helped the Vikings compile a 97–59–4 record in "The Met" against their often-shivering opponents. The fans, decked out in warm winter gear, loved it. But the NFL eventually declared Metropolitan Stadium's seating capacity too small, and in 1982, the Vikings moved indoors to the Metrodome. They developed a home-field advantage of a different sort when the screaming crowd would deafen opponents by using their outdoor voices. But in 2005, new Vikings owner Zygi Wilf expressed his view that the team should move back outside when its contract with the Metrodome expired after the 2011 season. In 2012, Vikings ownership and the state of Minnesota agreed to jointly build a new stadium (possibly with a retractable roof) by 2016.

BEFORE MOVING INDOORS IN 1982, THE VIKINGS EXCELLED IN WINTER WEATHER

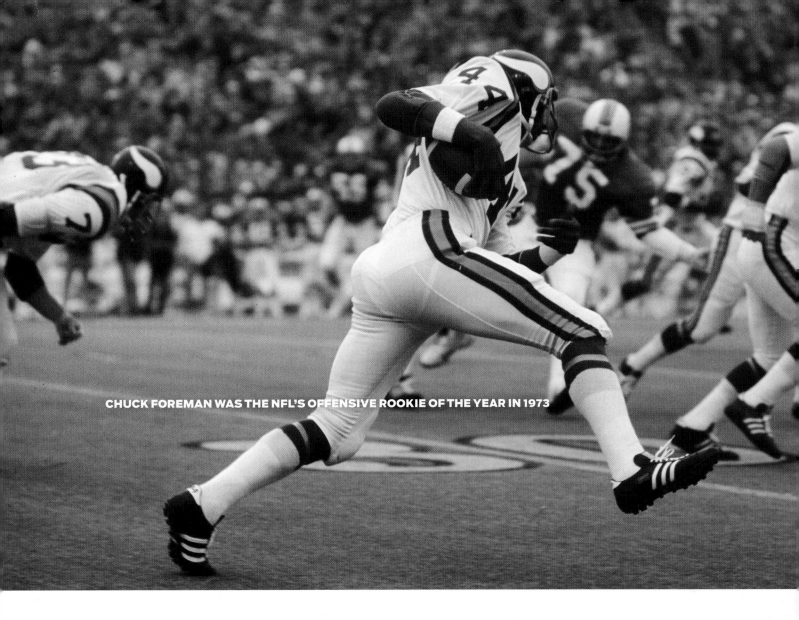

CHUCK FOREMAN WAS THE NFL'S OFFENSIVE ROOKIE OF THE YEAR IN 1973

zone as time expired, and the ball ricocheted off five different players before settling into the hands of receiver Ahmad Rashad, giving the Vikings an improbable 28–23 victory. The play became known in team lore as "The Miracle Catch."

The 1982 opening of the Hubert H. Humphrey Metrodome, an indoor stadium with a fiberglass roof, signaled the start of a new era for the Vikings. Old Metropolitan Stadium was torn down, and most of the team's former stars were soon replaced by a new band of Vikings. Despite the changes, Minnesota remained a mediocre team for most of the 1980s. Kramer quarterbacked the offense for many of those seasons, while the defense was led by linebacker Scott Studwell, tough safety Joey Browner, and defensive end Chris Doleman. Coach Grant intended to retire after the 1983 season, but after new coach

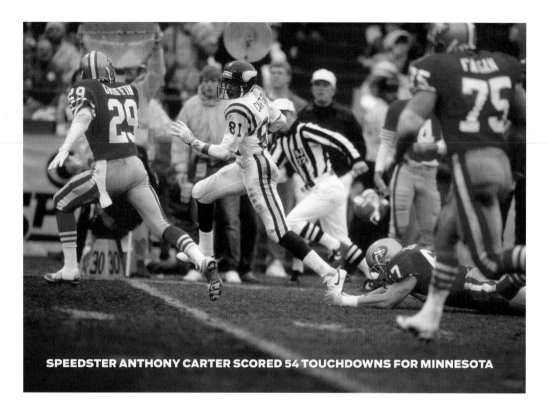

SPEEDSTER ANTHONY CARTER SCORED 54 TOUCHDOWNS FOR MINNESOTA

Les Steckel's 1984 team stumbled to a 3–13 mark, Grant returned for a final season in 1985 before stepping down for good.

Perhaps no Vikings player shone as brightly in the late '80s as receiver Anthony Carter. Carter joined Minnesota in 1985 after an amazing college career at the University of Michigan. Although he stood only 5-foot-11 and weighed just 169 pounds, Carter made up for his lack of size with terrific instincts and quickness. He also showed surprising speed, often streaking downfield to haul in long-range bombs. "I've always said that if the good Lord put anybody on this earth to play pro football, it was A. C.," said coach Jerry Burns, who took over for Grant in 1986. "He just forgot to give him a body."

Carter's heroics and a tough defense helped the Vikings make the playoffs in 1987, 1988, and 1989. In the 1987 postseason, the 8–7 Vikings stunned the sports world by beating the New Orleans Saints 44–10 and the San Francisco 49ers 36–24 to reach the NFC Championship Game. The title game against the Washington Redskins was a close battle, but Minnesota fell just short of the Super Bowl. The Vikings appeared ready to tie the game when Minnesota quarterback Wade Wilson fired a short pass to running back Darrin Nelson in the end zone late in the fourth quarter. But the ball slipped through Nelson's hands, giving the Redskins a 17–10 victory that propelled them to a Super Bowl title one game later.

Holding Court

After nine seasons as one of the most effective defensive tackles in the NFL, Alan Page was bored and thinking about retiring from football. He had already become the first defensive player to win the NFL MVP award and had played in three Super Bowls and was beginning to feel like there was nothing left to do. But then he landed on a different idea: attending law school. "The NFL wasn't my sole objective in life," Page said. "I had a wife and children. I knew I wasn't going to end up sitting on the beach somewhere when I was done playing." So instead of retiring, Page enrolled at the University of Minnesota Law School and took classes during the off-season. After graduating in 1978, he started working with a Minneapolis law firm during the off-season, where he specialized in labor law and served as an adviser to the NFL Players Association. When he decided to retire from football in 1981 after a distinguished 16-year career, he continued practicing law in Minneapolis and, in 1993, became a Minnesota Supreme Court Justice.

ALAN PAGE EARNED HIS LAW DEGREE WHILE PLAYING FOR THE VIKINGS

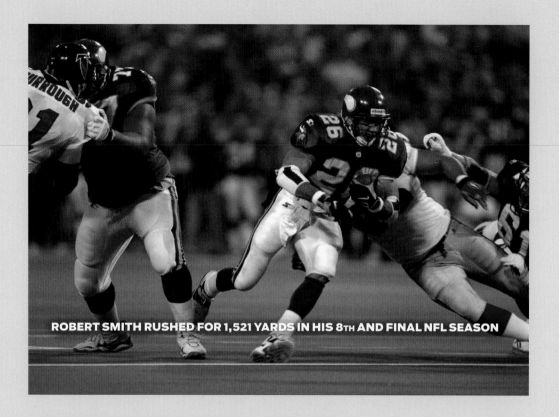

ROBERT SMITH RUSHED FOR 1,521 YARDS IN HIS 8TH AND FINAL NFL SEASON

The Green Era

In 1992, the Vikings brought in former Stanford University coach Dennis Green as their new leader. At the time, the Vikings were best known for their defense. Luckily, Minnesota had just acquired a player Coach Green could build a mighty offense around, too: wide receiver Cris Carter.

Carter had been a good player with the Philadelphia Eagles, but he had also struggled with drug and alcohol problems, and the Eagles cut him in 1990. Carter's lanky frame and terrific hands enabled him to catch virtually any pass, and his confident and vocal personality made him essentially a coach on the field. In 1994, he set a new NFL record with 122 catches, many of them on high, "alley-oop" passes. "I always tell the quarterback, when in doubt, just throw it high, and I'll go up and get it," Carter said.

Green and Carter led the Vikings back to power as Minnesota made the playoffs every year but one between 1992 and 2000, winning the NFC Central four times. A number of players contributed to these good times. Robert Smith, a long-striding running back with great speed, was drafted in 1993 and went on to average more than

SURE-HANDED RECEIVER CRIS CARTER LED THE NFL WITH 122 CATCHES IN 1994

John Randle

DEFENSIVE TACKLE / VIKINGS SEASONS: 1990–2000 / HEIGHT: 6-FOOT-1 / WEIGHT: 290 POUNDS

If pure energy could have been embodied on the NFL gridiron in the 1990s, it would have donned black face paint, worn a purple number 93 jersey, and doggedly chased down quarterbacks. It would have looked exactly like John Randle. A disruptive, duck-walking, body-slamming force who ran his mouth at opponents all game long, Randle was a quarterback's worst nightmare. From his position on the defense's interior line, Randle infused hustle and comedy into Vikings teams that usually featured powerful offense and shaky defense. Randle developed a coyote-roadrunner relationship with Green Bay Packers quarterback Brett Favre, whom he sacked numerous times. In a memorable television commercial, Randle chased a chicken wearing a number 4 Packers jersey across his lawn before a final scene that showed him grilling chicken for dinner. But for all his acting, Randle did have serious substance. He was a seven-time Pro-Bowler and finished his career with 137.5 sacks, the most of any defensive tackle in NFL history—quite an accomplishment for a player who went undrafted by the league in his first year of eligibility. In 2010, he was inducted into the Hall of Fame.

RANDALL CUNNINGHAM LED THE VIKINGS TO A 15–1 RECORD IN 1998

1,000 yards a season throughout the rest of the '90s. Various quarterbacks came and went during the Green era, but in 1994, veteran passer Warren Moon joined the Vikings and set a new team record by throwing for 4,264 yards. On the defensive side of the ball, powerful and eccentric tackle John Randle was a nightmare for opposing quarterbacks, while hard-hitting linebackers Jack Del Rio and Ed McDaniel punished ballcarriers.

Making the playoffs was one thing, but reaching the Super Bowl was another. The Vikings lost in the first round of the playoffs every year until 1997. Then, in one of the most thrilling games in franchise history, quarterback Randall Cunningham helped turn a 19–3 halftime deficit to the Giants into a stunning 23–22 victory. The Vikings were beaten a week later, but even better things were just around the corner.

In 1998, the Vikings franchise was bought by Texas billionaire Red McCombs. The new owner introduced "Purple Pride" as the team's new battle cry, and he boldly predicted that Minnesota would go a perfect 16–0. Fortunately, the Vikings had just added a rookie receiver who would almost make that forecast a reality: Randy Moss. Moss stood 6-foot-4, and his otherworldly speed and jumping ability had

earned him the nickname "The Freak." "Moss is the scariest man in football and the best player, talent-wise," Green Bay Packers coach Mike Sherman said. "You hold your breath every time they snap the ball."

The Vikings didn't go 16–0 as McCombs had thought, but they came close. The 1998 Vikings went 15–1 and set a new NFL record with 556 total points on the season. Moss was especially spectacular, posting 1,313 receiving yards and scoring 17 receiving touchdowns—the latter a new league record for a rookie. In the playoffs, the Vikings crushed the Arizona Cardinals 41–21 to reach the NFC Championship Game.

Playing in front of a deafening Metrodome crowd, the Vikings raced to a 20–7 lead over the Atlanta Falcons.

AS A ROOKIE, RANDY MOSS BURST UPON THE SCENE WITH 17 TOUCHDOWN CATCHES

High-Powered Heartbreak

The 1998 Vikings offense had it all: a powerful line, the rushing of former track star Robert Smith, and a passing game featuring rejuvenated quarterback Randall Cunningham, sure-handed receiver Cris Carter, and fleet-footed rookie phenom Randy Moss. Even the Vikings' kicker, Gary Anderson, couldn't miss—he became the first NFL kicker to post a perfect season, not missing any of his 35 attempted field goals or 59 extra-point kicks. In all, the offensive juggernaut scored a then league-record 556 points and breezed through the regular season with a 15–1 mark. The Vikings thumped the Arizona Cardinals 41–21 in the first round of the playoffs and prepared to down the Atlanta Falcons to reach the Super Bowl. But the Falcons, 11-point underdogs, would not be blown out. Anderson had a 38-yard field goal try in the fourth quarter to seal the victory, but he finally missed a kick, and the Falcons forced overtime and converted a field goal for a 30–27 win. "Our offense was supposed to have been so explosive," said Moss, who had just one catch after halftime. "But we just couldn't make it happen in the clutch."

AS PAINFUL AS A VIKINGS LOSS CAN BE, MINNESOTA FANS ARE STALWART

CHRIS HOVAN RACKED UP 17 SACKS IN HIS 5 SEASONS IN MINNESOTA

But Minnesota's offense then sputtered, and the Falcons clawed their way back to tie the game at 27–27. In sudden-death overtime, Atlanta stopped the Vikings' offense before kicking a game-winning field goal. The Vikings and their fans were devastated. "The Super Bowl is something you dream of as a kid," Moss said sadly, "and we had an opportunity to get there.… We let it slip right out of our hands." The Vikings had reached the Super Bowl four times only to lose it in the 1970s, but this loss might have been the most disappointing ever for fans of the purple and gold.

Minnesota rebounded from the painful defeat by making the playoffs again the next two seasons. In 2000, behind the great play of young quarterback Daunte Culpepper—a 6-foot-4 and 260-pound threat to either launch the ball deep downfield or steamroller linebackers or defensive backs—Minnesota fought its way back to the NFC Championship Game. But in one of the worst performances in team history, the Vikings were obliterated 41–0 by the Giants. Soon after this embarrassing loss, a number of key leaders left town or retired. Among the departures were Minnesota's all-time rushing leader (Robert Smith), its all-time pass-catching leader (Cris Carter), and Coach Green.

A new era dawned as Mike Tice, a former Vikings tight end, was named the team's head coach. Tice instituted a new offensive strategy for the 2002 season called "The Randy Ratio," which called for Moss, the team's brightest star, to touch the ball on at least 40 percent of all offensive plays. Unfortunately, the plan fell flat as opposing teams focused on stopping Moss, who had an impressive 106 catches but only 7 touchdowns in the Vikings' 6–10 season.

LINEBACKER HENRI CROCKETT BOLSTERED THE VIKINGS' DEFENSE IN 2002 AND 2003

OPPOSING DEFENSES STRUGGLED TO COVER THE FLAMBOYANT MOSS (#84)

Purple Pride

With an offense that featured Moss and Culpepper, the Vikings remained a dangerous team in the new NFC North Division (which was formed in 2002). In 2004, Culpepper enjoyed a career year, setting Vikings single-season records for passing with 4,717 total yards and 39 touchdowns, and setting an NFL record for total yards running and passing with 5,123. Minnesota made the playoffs despite a mediocre 8–8 record, then traveled to Green Bay to face the archrival Packers and their star quarterback, Brett Favre.

Although Green Bay had a near-perfect playoff record at home and had won both games during the regular season against Minnesota, that contest turned into one of the most satisfying Vikings victories in years. Minnesota earned a lopsided 31–17 win, but Moss again stole headlines in a performance that epitomized his Vikings career. After making a late fourth-quarter touchdown catch, he taunted the Packers crowd by pretending to lower his pants and show his backside. That was to be Moss's final

DAUNTE CULPEPPER WAS THE VIKINGS' STARTING QUARTERBACK FOR FIVE SEASONS

✕Cris Carter

WIDE RECEIVER / VIKINGS SEASONS: 1990–2001 / HEIGHT: 6-FOOT-3 / WEIGHT: 202 POUNDS

Cris Carter's career almost ended before it even had a chance to begin. Carter came into the NFL out of Ohio State University with some baggage because he had been ruled ineligible for his senior season after having secretly signed with an agent. The Philadelphia Eagles picked him up in the NFL Draft and used him somewhat sparingly, even though Carter showed a knack for getting into the end zone, with 19 of his 89 career receptions as an Eagles player going for scores. In the 1990 preseason, Eagles coach Buddy Ryan cut Carter, saying, "All he does is catch touchdowns." That didn't sound so bad to the Minnesota Vikings, who claimed him for just a $100 waiver fee. In Minnesota, Carter turned his life around—freeing himself from substance abuse problems and becoming deeply religious—and earned a reputation for his acrobatic sideline catches and clutch, third-down receptions. With his sure hands, he continued to do what he did best—catch touchdowns. Carter finished his career with 130 touchdowns, placing him among the top 10 receivers of all time.

noteworthy game in a purple jersey. After the Vikings lost in the next round to the Philadelphia Eagles, Minnesota grew tired of the star receiver's disruptive antics and traded him to the Oakland Raiders.

After a disappointing 2005 campaign, both Culpepper and Coach Tice were shown the door by new team owner Zygi Wilf. Former Eagles assistant coach Brad Childress was hired as the new head coach. His first season at the helm yielded just a 6–10 record, but in 2007, the Vikings defense, led by cornerback Antoine Winfield, showed signs of dominance. The team contended for a postseason berth until the final week of the season, finishing with an 8–8 mark.

Although the Vikings' 2007 season ended shy of the playoffs, it did showcase a new offensive weapon who became an instant sensation: rookie running back Adrian

KEVIN WILLIAMS'S DEFENSIVE PLAY REMINDED FANS OF BYGONE DAYS

Peterson. A former star at the University of Oklahoma, Peterson boasted a rare combination of power, cutting ability, and breakaway speed. By the end of the year, he had become the new face of the franchise and earned NFL Offensive Rookie of the Year honors.

Before the start of the 2008 season, the Vikings made headlines by trading for Kansas City Chiefs defensive end Jared Allen, the NFL's sacks leader in 2007. With the relentless Allen placed alongside Pro Bowl tackles Kevin Williams and Pat Williams, Vikings fans started dreaming of a return to the days of the Purple People Eaters. The confident Allen was direct in stating his goals upon arrival, saying, "We expect to go to the Super Bowl." Allen then backed up his words by notching 14.5 sacks as the 2008 Vikings went 10–6 and won their first NFC North title. In the playoffs, though, neither Allen nor Peterson—who was crowned the NFL's rushing champ with 1,760 yards—could lift Minnesota above Philadelphia, as the Vikings lost, 26–14.

The Vikings made headlines again before the beginning of the 2009 season by signing their longtime nemesis, 39-year-old quarterback Brett Favre. Favre had led Green Bay to two Super Bowl appearances in the 1990s and was looking forward to getting back to the big game at the end of his career. Minnesota fans quickly fell in love with the hard-throwing quarterback—especially after he posted the most impressive stats of his career and led the Vikings back to the playoffs with a 12–4 record. Favre and first-year

Training Camp Tragedy

Six years into his career as an offensive tackle for the Vikings, Korey Stringer was finally developing into the dominant player Minnesota had hoped for when it had drafted him in 1995 out of Ohio State University. But on July 31, 2001, that development stopped forever. The 6-foot-5 and 350-pound Stringer, fighting his poor fitness level, weight, and an especially wicked late-summer heat wave, suffered heatstroke and collapsed at the Vikings' training camp in Mankato, Minnesota. He was taken to a medical tent and later rushed to a hospital but never responded to cool-down treatment. Stringer died early the next morning, leaving his family, teammates, and Minnesota fans in shock. The temperature was 90-plus degrees with high humidity, but NFL players had often dealt with such weather conditions. "It's hot everywhere," said Vikings receiver Cris Carter. "That's why they call it the dog days of summer. There's certain things you can't explain." Since the incident, teams league-wide have taken better heat precautions by practicing in light-colored uniforms, making water and shade more readily available, and always having a doctor on the field.

KOREY STRINGER EARNED A PRO BOWL TRIP THE SEASON BEFORE HIS DEATH

POWERHOUSE ADRIAN PETERSON QUICKLY BECAME ONE OF THE NFL'S BEST BACKS

PERCY HARVIN WAS A TRIPLE THREAT AS A RECEIVER, RUSHER, AND RETURNER

wide receiver Percy Harvin, who earned NFL Offensive Rookie of the Year honors, took the team all the way to the NFC Championship Game against the New Orleans Saints but lost on an overtime field goal, 31–28.

Although Favre returned for a second season in Minnesota, neither he nor the Vikings could recapture the magic of the previous season. Favre struggled with injuries all season and finally had to sit out a game in December, bringing an end to his record-setting string of 297 consecutive starts in 20 seasons. Harvin battled migraines that hampered his performance in 2010 as well.

But in the midst of working through injuries and transitioning to a new coach named at midseason (after Childress was fired), the Vikings also had to deal with Mother Nature. After several heavy snowfalls in November and December, the roof of the Metrodome collapsed early on the morning of December 12, forcing the Vikings to find new fields on which to play their final two home games. When the season finally ended, the Vikings had fallen to 6–10 and missed the playoffs.

The Metrodome roof was repaired by the start of the 2011 season, but the Vikings, led by veteran quarterback Donovan McNabb, weren't back up to snuff. After losing five of their first six games, McNabb was benched in favor of rookie Christian Ponder. Then Peterson went down with a high ankle sprain in Week 10 and tore his knee ligament in December. The injuries prevented him from recording a 1,000-yard season for the first time in his career. The Vikings finished out of playoff contention at 3–13,

Adrian Peterson

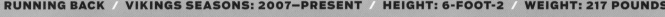

RUNNING BACK / VIKINGS SEASONS: 2007—PRESENT / HEIGHT: 6-FOOT-2 / WEIGHT: 217 POUNDS

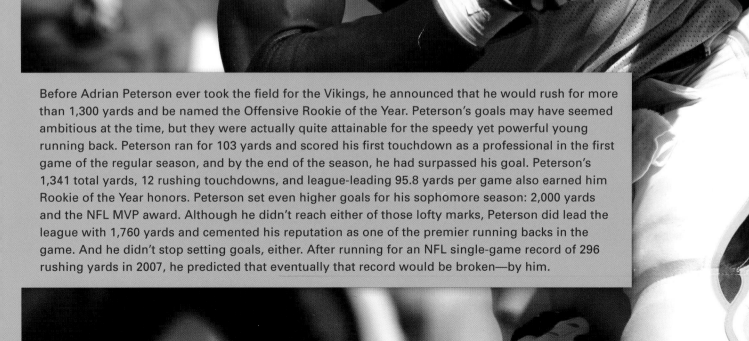

Before Adrian Peterson ever took the field for the Vikings, he announced that he would rush for more than 1,300 yards and be named the Offensive Rookie of the Year. Peterson's goals may have seemed ambitious at the time, but they were actually quite attainable for the speedy yet powerful young running back. Peterson ran for 103 yards and scored his first touchdown as a professional in the first game of the regular season, and by the end of the season, he had surpassed his goal. Peterson's 1,341 total yards, 12 rushing touchdowns, and league-leading 95.8 yards per game also earned him Rookie of the Year honors. Peterson set even higher goals for his sophomore season: 2,000 yards and the NFL MVP award. Although he didn't reach either of those lofty marks, Peterson did lead the league with 1,760 yards and cemented his reputation as one of the premier running backs in the game. And he didn't stop setting goals, either. After running for an NFL single-game record of 296 rushing yards in 2007, he predicted that eventually that record would be broken—by him.

THE VIKINGS TOOK SAFETY HARRISON SMITH IN THE FIRST ROUND OF THE 2012 DRAFT

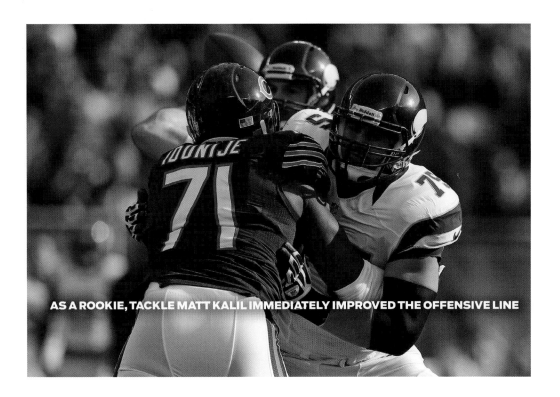

AS A ROOKIE, TACKLE MATT KALIL IMMEDIATELY IMPROVED THE OFFENSIVE LINE

their worst record since 1984. Their once dominant offense suddenly looked lackluster.

Peterson's remarkable comeback from knee surgery dominated the Vikings' 2012 season. After a rather quiet first five games, Peterson unleashed the beast in Week 6, rushing for 153 yards as Minnesota lost to the Redskins. From that point on, he chased the 2,000-yard mark, becoming the 7th running back in NFL history to achieve at least 2,000 yards in a season in the final game of 2012. His 2,097 total came tantalizingly close to breaking the record of 2,105 yards that had been set by Los Angeles Rams back Eric Dickerson in 1984. The other members of Minnesota's offensive squad did not keep pace with Peterson, especially after Harvin went down with an ankle injury at midseason. Nevertheless, Peterson's dynamic play carried the team to a 10–6 record and a Wild Card playoff against the rival Packers. Although the Vikings failed to advance any farther into the playoffs, fans rejoiced when Peterson was awarded the Offensive Player of the Year award in February 2013.

Whether their season ends in heartbreak or success, the Minnesota Vikings know that their fans are more numerous than the lakes in Minnesota and that they'll be there for them through thick and thin. The fans who enjoyed cheering their team on to four Super Bowl appearances—and a whole new generation of fans as well—are eager to root for the Vikings in many more Super Bowl games. Soon, they hope to welcome them home as champions.

DATE DUE

JUL 3 0 2016			
11-7-16			
			PRINTED IN U.S.A.